D1231621

J 929.92 Mar
Marcovitz, Hal
Confederate flag :
  controversial symbol of
  the south
                          $20.95
                  ocn868150618
                   08/04/2015

Confederate Flag

Controversial Symbol of the South

Confederate Flag
Controversial Symbol
of the South

Hal Marcovitz

Mason Crest
Philadelphia

Mason Crest
450 Parkway Drive, Suite D
Broomall, PA 19008
www.masoncrest.com

© 2015 by Mason Crest, an imprint of National Highlights, Inc.

All rights reserved. No part of this publication may be reproduced or transmitted in any form or by any means, electronic or mechanical, including photocopying, recording, taping, or any information storage and retrieval system, without permission from the publisher.

Printed and bound in the United States of America.

CPSIA Compliance Information: Batch #PSA2014. For further information, contact Mason Crest at 1-866-MCP-Book.

Publisher's note: all quotations in this book come from original sources, and contain the spelling and grammatical inconsistencies of the original text.

First printing
1 3 5 7 9 8 6 4 2

Library of Congress Cataloging-in-Publication Data

on file at the Library of Congress

ISBN: 978-1-4222-3121-0 (hc)
ISBN: 978-1-4222-8744-6 (ebook)

Patriotic Symbols of America series ISBN: 978-1-4222-3117-3

Contents

KEY ICONS TO LOOK FOR:

Text-dependent questions: These questions send the reader back to the text for more careful attention to the evidence presented there.

Words to understand: These words with their easy-to-understand definitions will increase the reader's understanding of the text, while building vocabulary skills.

Series glossary of key terms: This back-of-the book glossary contains terminology used throughout this series. Words found here increase the reader's ability to read and comprehend higher-level books and articles in this field.

Research projects: Readers are pointed toward areas of further inquiry connected to each chapter. Suggestions are provided for projects that encourage deeper research and analysis.

Sidebars: This boxed material within the main text allows readers to build knowledge, gain insights, explore possibilities, and broaden their perspectives by weaving together additional information to provide realistic and holistic perspectives.

Patriotic Symbols and American History

Symbols are not merely ornaments to admire—they also tell us stories. If you look at one of them closely, you may want to find out why it was made and what it truly means. If you ask people who live in the society in which the symbol exists, you will learn some things. But by studying the people who created that symbol and the reasons why they made it, you will understand the deepest meanings of that symbol.

The United States owes its identity to great events in history, and the most remarkable of our patriotic symbols are rooted in these events. The struggle for independence from Great Britain gave America the Declaration of Independence, the Liberty Bell, the American flag, and other images of freedom. The War of 1812 gave the young country a song dedicated to the flag, "The Star-Spangled Banner," which became our national anthem. Nature gave the country its national animal, the bald eagle. These symbols established the identity of the new nation, and set it apart from the nations of the Old World.

To be emotionally moving, a symbol must strike people with a sense of power and unity. But it often takes a long time for a new symbol to be accepted by all the people, especially if there are older symbols that have gradually lost popularity. For example, the image of Uncle Sam has replaced Brother Jonathan, an earlier representation of the national will, while the Statue of Liberty has replaced Columbia, a woman who represented liberty to Americans in the early 19th century. Since then, Uncle Sam and the Statue of Liberty have endured and have become cherished icons of America.

Of all the symbols, the Statue of Liberty has perhaps the most curious story, for unlike other symbols, Americans did not create her. She was created by the French, who then gave her to America. Hence, she represented not what Americans thought of their country but rather what the French thought of America. It was many years before Americans decided to accept this French goddess of Liberty as a symbol for the United States and its special role among the nations: to spread freedom and enlighten the world.

This series of books is valuable because it presents the story of each of America's great symbols in a freshly written way and will contribute to the students' knowledge and awareness of them. It it to be hoped that this information will awaken an abiding interest in American history, as well as in the meanings of American symbols.

—Barry Moreno,
librarian and historian
Ellis Island/Statue of Liberty National Monument

Words to Understand

Confederacy—short for Confederate States of America, an organization of the 11 Southern states that seceded from the United States in 1860 and 1861.

delegate—a person designated to represent others, often at a political meeting or convention.

vessel—a large ship.

The crew of the Confederate steamship *Shenandoah* were the last Confederates to surrender at the end of the Civil War. General Robert E. Lee surrendered his army while the ship was at sea, and the sailors on the *Shenandoah* did not receive the news until they were told by a passing British ship.

Voyage of the *Shenandoah*

T he *Sea King* was a fast steamship that arrived in the Madeira Islands off the coast of Africa in October 1864. It had left London 10 days before. Along the way the ship met a supply ship carrying guns and ammunition. Also on board was Captain James Waddell, an officer in the navy of the Confederate States of America.

In port in Madeira, Waddell's job was to turn the *Sea King* into a fighting **vessel** in the Confederate Navy. He would then take over as the ship's commander. Waddell supervised the placement of guns and ammunition aboard the *Sea King* and made the ship ready for combat. He also renamed the *Sea King*. It became known as the Confederate States Ship (C.S.S.) *Shenandoah*.

When the ship and crew were ready, Waddell guided the *Shenandoah* west out of Madeira, across the Atlantic

Ocean toward the coast of New England. Its mission was to sink whaling ships that were heading home with their rich cargoes of whale fat, called blubber.

High atop one of the *Shenandoah's* masts flew the ship's colors—its battle flag. Known as the Confederate Navy Jack, it included the Southern Cross flag. This consisted of a blue cross containing 13 stars set against a red field. The Southern Cross flag had been carried into battle by Confederate soldiers since early in the war. In the navy flag, the Southern Cross flag was set on a white background.

The hunting was good for the *Shenandoah*. Waddell's ship sank six Union vessels in a little more than three weeks of sailing. On November 12, 1864, the *Shenandoah* turned south and headed toward South America. Along the way, Waddell's ship encountered three more Union vessels and sank them all. By the end of 1864, the *Shenandoah* had sailed around Cape Horn on the tip of South America and headed north. Its captain intended to sink Union whaling ships bound for Hawaii.

Despite the *Shenandoah's* success at sea, the Civil War was drawing to an end. On April 9, 1865, General Robert E. Lee, commander of the Confederate Army, surrendered to General Ulysses S. Grant at Appomattox Court House in Virginia. Although some Confederates continued to fight, the conflict was essentially over.

Captain Waddell had no idea the war had ended. During April, May, and June the *Shenandoah* continued its attacks on whaling ships in the Pacific Ocean, wreaking havoc on merchant shipping.

On June 22, while sailing north of Japan in the Bering Sea, the *Shenandoah* encountered the whaler *Jerah Swift*, which was based in New Bedford, Massachusetts. The *Shenandoah* fired one of its big cannons at the *Jerah Swift* and scored a direct hit. Waddell had no idea that he had just fired the final shot in the Civil War.

Several weeks later, the crew of a merchant ship stopped by the *Shenandoah* showed Captain Waddell a newspaper story about the surrender of the **Confederacy**. When he read the news, Waddell sailed for England in an effort to avoid capture by the U.S. Navy. On November 6, 1865—seven months after the surrender of General Lee— the *Shenandoah* arrived at Liverpool, England, still flying the Confederate flag. The flag was lowered. It would never again fly as the official flag of a nation.

"I claim for her officers and men a triumph over their enemies and over every obstacle," Captain Waddell wrote. "For myself, I claim having done my duty."

Text-Dependent Question
Who was the captain of the C.S.S. *Shenandoah*?

Research Project
The *Shenandoah*'s mission was to attack whaling ships, not American warships. Explain why Confederate leaders proposed this strategy, and what they hoped would occur as a result.

Words to Understand

bunting—a lightweight fabric used for flags and decorations.

capital—the city that serves as official center of government for a state or nation.

Capitol—a building located in the capital where the government passes laws and conducts other business.

Congress—the lawmaking branch of the federal government.

constellation—a group of stars that forms a familiar pattern.

halyard—rope used to hoist a flag up a pole.

president—the chief executive of a country whose authority to govern is provided by vote of the citizens.

seamstress—a woman whose occupation is sewing.

secede—to withdraw from an organization.

The first president of the Confederate States of America, Jefferson Davis, is pictured with his advisors in Montgomery, Alabama, in this illustration made in February 1861. The man standing on the left is Christopher G. Memminger, who contributed to the design of several Confederate flags.

The Stars and Bars

The notion that the Confederacy would need its own flag was raised in Montgomery, Alabama, in February 1861, as *delegates* from Southern states that had decided to leave the Union gathered to write a charter for their new government.

The Confederate *Congress* met in the Alabama State House. Jefferson Davis had just been elected the first *president* of the Confederacy. He appointed a committee to design a Great Seal, Coat of Arms, motto, and flag. William Porcher Miles, a delegate from South Carolina, was made chairman of what became known as the Flag and Seal Committee.

The committee soon found itself swamped with ideas. The first designs were proposed by Christopher G.

Memminger, a delegate from South Carolina. One of Memminger's designs called for a blue cross of seven stars on a red field. Memminger said the design was based on the *constellation* known as the Southern Cross. The stars stood for the seven states that sent delegates to the Confederate Congress—South Carolina, Mississippi, Florida, Alabama, Georgia, Louisiana and Texas.

Memminger submitted similar designs that contained as many as 15 stars to represent the slave-holding states that had not sent delegates to the Confederate Congress—Virginia, Arkansas, Tennessee and North Carolina, as well as Maryland, which attempted to *secede* but was prevented by federal troops to ensure the safety of the federal *capital* in Washington, D.C.; Delaware, a slave state that remained loyal to the Union; and Kentucky and Missouri, which had both Confederate and Union governments. Memminger said it was his hope every slave state would soon join in "the glorious constellation of our Southern Confederacy."

Miles and the other members of the flag committee were not prepared to accept Memminger's designs. Some members of the Confederate Congress saw no reason the Confederacy should not adopt the Stars and Stripes as the flag as well as the "The Star-Spangled Banner" by Francis Scott Key as the national anthem of the South. President Davis and many delegates to the Confederate Congress believed the South had just as much right as the North to the Stars and Stripes flag.

Over the next month the flag committee received proposed designs for the new flag from several delegates.
Eventually, Miles and the other committee members
found themselves considering some 120 designs for the
new flag. The flag committee rejected all the designs submitted by the delegates and decided to look elsewhere.
In its report to the Confederate Congress, the committee
wrote: "A flag should be simple, readily made, and,
above all, capable of being made up in *bunting*; it should
be different from the flag of any other country, place or
people; it should be significant; it should be readily
distinguishable at a distance; the colors should be well
contrasted and durable; and lastly, and not the least

VITAL FIGURE: William P. Miles

William Porcher Miles, a deputy to the Confederate Congress from
South Carolina, was appointed by Confederate President Jefferson
Davis to head the Flag and Seal Committee. His committee eventually
approved the design for the Stars and Bars. Later, while serving on the
staff of General Beauregard, Miles helped design the Southern Cross
battle flag.

He was born in 1822 in Waterloo, South Carolina, and graduated
from the College of Charleston in South Carolina in 1842. In 1855, he
was elected mayor of Charleston. Miles was elected to the U.S. Congress
in 1857, where he supported slavery and secession. He left Washington
in 1860.

In 1863, Miles married Betty Beirne, daughter of Oliver Beirne, a
wealthy owner of plantations in Virginia and Louisiana. Following the
war, Miles managed his father-in-law's plantations in Louisiana, over-
seeing them and living quietly until his death in 1899.

important point, it should be effective and handsome."

The flag the committee finally picked was not that much different from the Stars and Stripes.

Mrs. Napoleon Lockett, the daughter of Alabama Governor Andrew B. Moore, knew an artist and teacher named Niccola Marschall who lived in nearby Marion, Alabama. She asked Marschall to propose a design. The artist quickly sketched three designs, one of which showed three wide horizontal stripes of equal width. The two outer stripes were red while the inside stripe was white. In the upper left corner he placed a field of blue with a circle of seven stars. Mrs. Lockett showed it to the committee. There was no question the Marschall design bore considerable similarity to Old Glory. However, the design was quickly adopted as the first

This sheet music for a song about the Confederate Flag was dedicated to Confederate president Jefferson Davis. Written in early 1861, the cover features the newly designed "Stars and Bars" flag of the Confederacy.

official flag of the Confederate States of America.

The first Confederate flag was sewn March 2 by a *seamstress* in Montgomery, Alabama. The committee's plan was to unveil the new flag—which became known as the Stars and Bars—on March 4, 1861, the day Abraham Lincoln would take the oath of office as president of the United States in Washington, D.C.

On that day, a huge crowd gathered outside the Alabama State House. President Davis decided to give the honor of raising the first flag of the Confederacy to Letitia C. Tyler, the granddaughter of former U.S. President John Tyler, who had been a delegate to the Confederate Congress.

At just past 4 P.M., a brass band started to play the anthem of the Confederacy, "Dixie." Standing below a flagpole on the *Capitol* grounds, Letitia drew down on the *halyard*, and the Stars and Bars flag was hoisted over the cheering crowd.

> ## Make Connections
>
> The first ship to fly the Stars and Bars flag following secession was the *Pearl*, which sailed for Antigua on March 5, 1861. When the ship arrived in port, angry sailors from New England tore the Stars and Bars from its mast.

Text-Dependent Question
What was the first capital of the Confederacy?

Research Project
What were the first seven states that agreed to form the Confederate States of America? How many other states later voted to secede and join the Confederacy?

Words to Understand

casualties—soldiers wounded, captured, or killed in battle.

regiment—a military unit of infantry or cavalry soldiers.

masthead—the print across the top of a newspaper's front page that displays the newspaper's name.

strategies—a series of plans intended to complete a wide-scale military maneuver.

tactics—maneuvers designed to position a military force for a specific attack.

Union and Confederate troops clash at the Battle of Franklin, Tennessee, in November 1864. Soon after the Civil War began, the Confederates adopted a new flag to carry into battle, featuring a blue cross with thirteen white stars on a red background. This battle flag, also known as the Southern Cross, has become the most recognizable symbol of the Confederacy.

The Southern Cross

Within days, the new Stars and Bars flag was flying across the Confederacy. Hastily made copies were stitched together and flown over the capital buildings of the rebellious states. Ships anchored in Confederate harbors flew the flag atop their masts. Newspapers published in the South featured images of the flag on their *mastheads*. In Montgomery, Alabama, the Confederate Congress ordered an enormous version made for the Capitol measuring 28 feet by 18 feet.

Early in the morning of April 12—just five weeks after the flag was hoisted over the Capitol in Montgomery—southern troops fired on a Union force guarding Fort Sumter in the harbor of Charleston, South Carolina. The first shots of the Civil War had been launched. Soon armies wearing Union blue or Confederate gray would clash during four years of bloody, tragic fighting.

The attack on Fort Sumter was led by a Confederate general named Pierre Gustave Toutant Beauregard. The soldiers inside the fort withstood bombardment from Beauregard's guns for nearly two days, then surrendered. Beauregard emerged from the short battle as the first hero of the Confederacy.

VITAL FIGURE: General P.T.G. Beauregard

General Pierre Beauregard was one of the first heroes of the South—he commanded the artillery brigade that bombarded Fort Sumter with cannon shots, thus touching off the Civil War in April 1861. Months later, at the Battle of First Manassas, he was instrumental in routing the Union Army, delivering the South's first important victory.

Beauregard was born in St. Bernard Parish, Louisiana. He was trained as a soldier at the U.S. Military Academy at West Point and fought in the Mexican War during the late 1840s. He resigned from the U.S. Army in 1861 to join the Confederate Army.

Not all his battles during the Civil War were Southern victories. He lost the important Battle of Shiloh, and was relieved of command of the Confederate Army in Tennessee. He was placed in charge of troops defending the coastlines of Georgia and South Carolina. Late in the war Beauregard was again given command of an army, and helped slow the advance of the Union Army toward Richmond, Virginia.

Following the war, Beauregard returned to Louisiana and became president of a railroad. He died in New Orleans in 1893.

Two months later, the armies of the North and South clashed near Manassas, Virginia. Unlike Fort Sumter, in which no one injured or killed, Manassas was a bloody battle that featured many *casualties*. Thousands of soldiers on foot and horseback slammed into each other on July 21, 1861.

Generals found themselves in the field directing *strategies* and *tactics*. One of those generals was Beauregard. His troops were pinned down along a road known as the Warrenton Turnpike. In front of Beauregard's troops was a large force of Union soldiers. General Beauregard wanted to attack, but he needed more men to hold his position while his soldiers charged the Union lines. Late in the afternoon, Beauregard received a dispatch from his signal officer, Captain Edward P. Alexander, reporting an approaching force of soldiers in the rear. Unfortunately, they were flying a red, white, and blue flag. Alexander said he could not tell whether it was the Stars and Bars, or if they were Northern troops.

There was little breeze, meaning the banners carried by the troops hung straight and lifeless. What's more, the dust kicked up by the troops, wagons and horses obscured everyone's vision.

Soon, General Beauregard could see the approaching soldiers for himself. Unfortunately, he could not identify whether they were Union or Confederate soldiers, either.

"General Beauregard tried again and again to decide

This 19th century illustration shows Union troops charging the Confederate lines at Manassas. Note the similarities in the American flag at left and in the Confederate Stars and Bars flag at the right.

what colors they carried," wrote Carlton McCarthy, a private in the Confederate Army. "He used his glass repeatedly, and handing it to others begged them to look, hoping their eyes might be keener than his."

Beauregard had to make a decision. Should he hold his ground on the chance the troops were on his side? Or should he order a withdrawal? If he remained, and the troops turned out to be Union, his men would surely be caught in a trap between the two large Northern armies.

"Suddenly, a puff of wind spread the colors to the

breeze," wrote McCarthy. "It was the Confederate flag—the Stars and Bars. The moment the flag was recognized, Beauregard turned to his staff, right and left, saying, 'See that the day is ours!' and ordered an immediate advance."

The Confederate forces charged into the Union lines. Beauregard's attack helped turn the tide that day in favor of the South, which won what would come to be known as the First Battle of Manassas. It is also called the First Battle of Bull Run. A second battle took place at the same place in August 1862.

Manassas may have been a great victory for the South, but Beauregard knew that it could have been a defeat if he had guessed wrong about the color of the approaching flag. Clearly, he knew, the Southern troops would need a distinctive and colorful banner to carry onto the battlefields against the Union soldiers. He discussed the issue with other Confederate military leaders. They agreed that a different flag was needed.

Beauregard proposed a new battle flag similar to the banner suggested by Christopher Memminger some months before. Other generals learned of Beauregard's plans and recommended designs as well. Finally, Beauregard had his

Make Connections

Ironically, the United States supplied the material for a lot of the South's flags. Many Confederate battle flags were sewn from a supply of red fabric captured from a warehouse at the Navy base in Norfolk, Virginia early in the war.

regiment's mapmaker draw a flag that depicted a banner with a blue cross, white stars, and a red field.

In their correspondence, Beauregard and the other generals referred to the new flag as "St. Andrew's Cross." St. Andrew, a follower of Jesus Christ, had been put to death by the Romans on a cross nailed together in the shape of an "X." The cross was also known as the saltire, and had been adopted as the flag of Scotland.

On the Confederate battle flag, the blue cross included 13 stars, even though at this point only 11 states had seceded from the Union. On the battle flag, the two extra stars represented Kentucky and Missouri. There was no question that the bold and brilliant red flag could be recognized in the field by soldiers on both sides of the battle, no matter how little wind there was, or how much dust was kicked up by the horses and wagons.

The War Department approved the change. Confederate soldiers would now go into battle under the Southern Cross. Officers and men of the Confederate army greeted the new flag with enthusiasm.

This is the Confederate battle flag, with its "southern cross" and 13 stars. During the Civil War many Confederate battle flags were square rather than rectangular; it was believed the square shape would save silk, which was hard to find in the South.

Meanwhile, the Confederate Congress had grown increasingly dissatisfied with the Stars and Bars. Both delegates and Confederate citizens complained that a flag of red and white stripes and cluster of stars on a blue field resembled the American flag—the emblem of a country they had grown to hate.

On May 1, 1863, the Confederate government replaced the Stars and Bars with a second national flag. The new flag was a white banner with the Southern Cross placed in the upper left corner.

VITAL FIGURE: Christopher Memminger

Christopher G. Memminger, a delegate to the Confederate Congress from South Carolina, had suggested a flag based on the Southern Cross. He was turned down by the flag committee, which instead approved the Stars and Bars. Later, his design found its way onto the Confederate Army's battle flags, and by the end of the Civil War the Southern Cross flag was the most recognizable symbol of the South.

After the war started, Memminger had little time to involve himself in the debate over the flag. Confederate President Jefferson Davis appointed him secretary of the treasury, meaning it was Memminger's responsibility to collect money to pay for the war.

He was able to raise money from citizens of the South by selling war bonds. The government of the Confederate States of America issued the bonds with the promise to repay the money with interest to the citizens after the war. Of course, the government did not survive the war, so people who bought the bonds had no way to get their money back.

Today, Confederate bonds are likely to be worth a lot of money to collectors, but many people who lived in the South during the war and supported the Confederate government lost their life savings by buying the bonds.

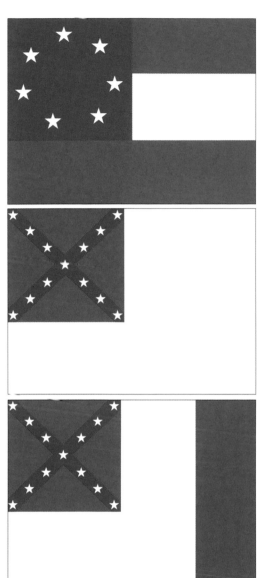

Three of the flags used by the Confederacy: The original Stars and Bars is on the top. The seven stars represent the seven states that initially voted to secede from the United States. A later version of this flag had a circle of 12 stars in the blue field, with a larger star in the center. In 1863 the Stars and Bars was replaced by the Stainless Banner, which featured the battle flag on a field of white. In the Confederacy's final flag, a vertical red stripe was added to the Stainless Banner; however, few of these flags were made because the Civil War ended about a month after this new flag was unveiled.

This flag was known as the "Stainless Banner." Some troops in the field adopted the new flag and carried it in battle, but when there was no wind and the flag drooped on its pole, it was difficult to see the Southern Cross. When this happened, the Stainless Banner appeared as nothing more than a white flag, which in battle is the flag of surrender.

In early 1865, even though the Civil War was nearly over, the Confederate Congress decided to create a new flag. This flag, adopted on March 8, 1865, was very similar to the Stainless Banner, but it now included a broad vertical red stripe along the outer edge of the banner.

Make Connections

General Thomas "Stonewall" Jackson died from a wound he received at the Battle of Chancellorsville; he was buried in Lexington, Kentucky, in a coffin draped with one of the Stainless Banners. After his funeral the Stainless Banner was sometimes referred to as the "Jackson Flag."

By now, though, the Civil War was just weeks away from its conclusion. After four years of war, there was little food, ammunition, or raw materials left in the South. Certainly, whatever fabrics were available were needed to make and mend clothes of the citizens and returning soldiers. Few copies of the final flag were stitched and displayed.

Text-Dependent Question

What Confederate general recommended that a new battle flag be adopted because the Stars and Bars design was too similar to the American flag?

Research Project

The number of stars on Confederate flags varied—some had seven stars, others had 11, 12, or 13. How many states were actually part of the Confederacy, and represented by stars on a Confederate flag? What did the other stars represent?

Words to Understand

anthem—a rousing or uplifting song identified with a particular country, organization, or cause.

The graves of Confederate soldiers are marked with flags in a Virginia cemetery. In the years following the war, citizens of both the North and the South set aside a day at the end of May to decorate soldiers' graves with flowers and flags. Originally called Decoration Day, it has become the national holiday on which we honor all those who have fought for the United States, Memorial Day.

"Dye It With Your Blood!"

By the end of 1861, the Southern Cross battle flag was a familiar sight at the head of Confederate armies. Many of those first flags did not feature red fields behind the cross of stars, but a pink or rose-colored background. When Confederate Army officers complained about the color to Beauregard, he barked: "Dye it red sir, dye it with your blood!"

The flag was often dyed with the blood of the flag bearer. It was a great honor to be chosen to carry the flag into battle, but it was also one of the most dangerous jobs in the regiment. The flag bearer was unable to carry a gun, and he found himself an easy target because enemy soldiers would aim for the flag.

VITAL FIGURES: The flag-making Cary sisters

According to Confederate legend, the first three Southern Cross battle flags were stitched by sisters Hetty and Jennie Cary of Baltimore, Maryland, and their cousin, Constance Cary, of Alexandria, Virginia. The Cary women are said to have sewn the flags from material they obtained by taking apart their fancy party dresses.

In later years, historians found letters written by Constance Cary, in which she describes the first flags made of red and blue silk, and how difficult it was to obtain the material. That would suggest the flags were not made from the ladies' dresses. They would be quite easy to find hanging in their closets.

In any event, it appears the Cary sisters and their cousin presented the first three flags to Generals Earl Van Dorn, Joseph Johnston, and Pierre Beauregard. When Van Dorn died during a battle in Tennessee, his flag was returned to Constance.

Hetty Cary spent the war years doing volunteer work in Richmond, Virginia, for the Confederate war effort. On January 19, 1865, Hetty married General John Pegram. Three weeks later, her new husband was killed in the Battle of Hatcher's Run.

One Confederate flag bearer, Lieutenant P. E. Drew, was described by his fellow soldiers as "rushing into the jaws of death." Drew had picked up the banner from his company's fallen flag bearer and was racing into the Union line when he was shot through the heart. At Gettysburg, 14 flag bearers from one North Carolina regiment lost their lives in the course of the battle.

Today, the term "Color Guard" usually refers to the high school or college students who march at the front of their school's band in a parade, accompanying the colors. During the Civil War, the Color Guard was made up of a group of soldiers—usually a sergeant and five or more corporals—whose job during the battle was to protect the flag bearer and the flag. Members of the Color Guard had dangerous jobs. Many of them were killed protecting their flags.

Troops watching the advance of an army toward them always looked for the flag. If the flag appeared to be bouncing up and down, they knew the enemy was advancing toward them on the run. They called this type of advance "on the double quick."

There was no standard Confederate battle flag issued to every regiment throughout the war. Generals often tinkered with the size and shape of the flag. Many regimental leaders preferred a square flag to a rectangular banner. Some officers had the names of battles sewn into the flags to commemorate important victories by their units. Some generals preferred a white border to the flag

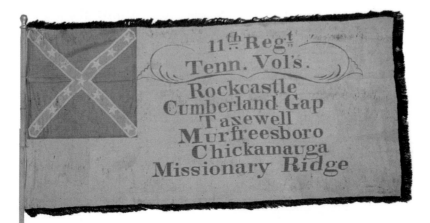

Each fighting unit of the Confederate Army had its own battle flag. This flag of the 11th Tennessee Regiment lists battles in which the regiment saw action.

while others favored an orange border. Sometimes, the stars were cut out of gold cloth.

General Stanhope Watie, the last Confederate general to surrender, had a flag made up that resembled the Stars and Bars, but the banner contained 16 stars in the blue field. Watie said the 16 stars stood for the 11 states that seceded from the Union and the five Indian nations that supported the South's war against the North. Across the central bar of the flag were the words "Cherokee Braves." Watie was three-quarters Cherokee and many members of his regiment were Indians.

Many states adopted what was known as the "Bonnie Blue Flag" during the war. This flag included just one large white star against a field of blue. Single-starred flags were displayed to show the state had cut its ties with the union. The name "Bonnie Blue" came from a

Belle Boyd had been a popular member of Washington society before the Civil War. During the war, she became a spy for the Confederacy, and displayed the flag outside her home in Virginia. On July 4, 1861, a group of Union soldiers spotted the flag and attempted to tear it down. They didn't get too far. Boyd shot the leader of the group, causing the other Union soldiers to flee. The Confederate flag remained in front of her home.

popular song named "Bonnie Blue" that was written and sung by a comedian named Harry McCarthy.

The Bonnie Blue flag.

Women across the South were drafted to stitch the flags. One factory in Richmond employed some 2,000 Confederate women to sew uniforms for the soldiers as well as battle flags.

Civilians in the South were often willing to put their lives on the line for the flag as well. After New Orleans was captured by Union troops, General Benjamin F. Butler ordered the people of the city not to display symbols of the Confederacy. One woman responded by sewing a dress from the battle flag; she then strolled through the streets of the city in defiance of Butler's order. Butler had her arrested and thrown in prison.

A Confederate spy named Rose Greenhow smuggled a flag into her prison cell in Washington. Greenhow was said to have waved the flag from her cell window every day she was held in custody.

 Text-Dependent Questions
What was the job of the flag bearer? Why was it dangerous?

 Research Project
Look up the lyrics of "The Bonnie Blue Flag." Do they present events leading up to the Civil War as they actually happened? If not, how do they differ?

Words to Understand

boycott—to refuse to deal with a person or group, in order to show disapproval or force acceptance of certain conditions.

centennial—a 100th anniversary.

legislature—the lawmaking branch of a state government.

referendum—a vote by the people on a law proposed by a government body.

In this photo taken in April 2000, the Confederate battle flag flies over the South Carolina statehouse beneath the American flag and the state flag of South Carolina. The South Carolina State Senate voted to remove the Confederate flag from atop the Capitol dome on April 14, 2000—exactly 139 years after the Stars and Bars had been hoisted over Fort Sumter by victorious rebel soldiers.

Hatred or Heritage?

Since the end of the Civil War, African Americans as well as others have regarded the Confederate flag as a symbol of hatred and racism. Over the years it has not been uncommon to see news reports on television that showed Confederate battle flags waved by members of the Ku Klux Klan, a racist organization. Opponents of the Confederate flag say that it is a shameful reminder of a dark period in the nation's history, when slavery of African Americans was legal

But many white citizens of the South do not regard the Confederate flag as a symbol of racism. They feel it is an important symbol of their history and heritage, and that the flag represents the bravery and sacrifices of ancestors who they feel fought for a noble cause.

Make Connections

Confederate battle flags captured by Union soldiers were held by the United States War Department until the early 1900s, when they were returned to the secessionist states.

In no place has the debate over the use of the Confederate flag been louder than in the states of Georgia, South Carolina, and Mississippi.

For years, the state flags of Georgia and Mississippi included images of the Confederate battle flag. In South Carolina, the battle flag flew atop the state Capitol dome right next to the state's official flag.

The story of Georgia's state flag dated back to July 1, 1956, when John Sammons Bell, a local political leader, convinced the state *legislature* to adopt a design for the flag that included an image of the state's official seal in a blue field on the inner third of the flag, while the rest of the flag contained an image of the Southern Cross battle flag. The Georgia flag also included the words "Wisdom, Justice, and Moderation."

But by the 1990s, black citizens of Georgia wanted to know why a symbol they considered racist should be allowed to fly over the state government's buildings. After several years of debate, black leaders in Georgia convinced the state legislature to adopt a new flag. Many descendants of Civil War veterans called on the legislature to resist the change, but, finally, on January 31, 2001, a new flag was hoisted over the Capitol. This design still featured an image of the Southern Cross, but on the new flag the cross was far less prominent than it had been before.

In 2003, the Georgia flag was re-designed again. The new flag does not include the Southern Cross. Instead, it resembles the Stars and Bars flag of the Confederacy. The blue field contains the state coat of arms inside a circle of 13 stars, which are meant to represent Georgia's place as one of the original American colonies.

Unlike Georgia, the state flag of South Carolina does not

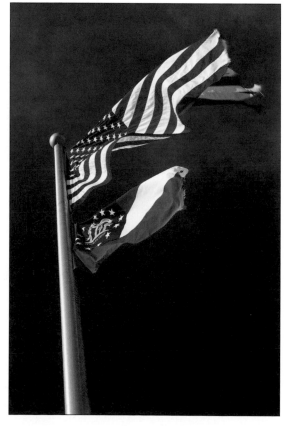

(Top) The Georgia state flag introduced in 2001 featured smaller versions of earlier Georgia flags, including one that contained the Confederate battle flag.

(Right) In May 2003, a new Georgia state flag was introduced. Here, it flies under the American flag.

include any similarities to Confederate flags. The South Carolina flag contains the images of a palmetto tree and crescent moon on a blue field. But in 1962, South Carolina legislators ordered the Confederate battle flag flown atop the Capitol dome alongside the state flag to mark the 100th anniversary of the Civil War. At the end of the *centennial*, the Southern Cross stayed atop the dome.

For years, members of the National Association for the Advancement of Colored People (NAACP) pressured South Carolina's legislators to take down the battle flag. In early 2000, the NAACP urged its members not to travel in South Carolina or take vacations there. South

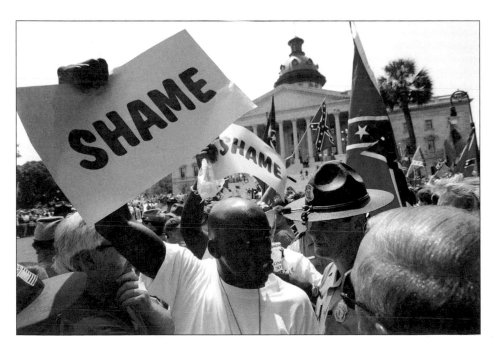

A man holds up a sign protesting the Confederate flag flying over the South Carolina statehouse in July 2000. A few moments after this photo was taken, the flag was officially removed from the government building. It now flies over a nearby cemetery.

Carolina gets a lot of money from tourists who visit the state's coastal towns and beaches. Tourism officials estimated that the NAACP *boycott* cost businesses in South Carolina millions of dollars a month.

South Carolina's political leaders finally relented, and on July 1, 2000, the Confederate flag came down from the Capitol dome. However, the flag's supporters did win a compromise, receiving approval to raise the battle flag over a nearby cemetery for Confederate soldiers. The flag still flies there, despite the continuation of the boycott by civil rights groups. In addition, the National Collegiate Athletic Association (NCAA) has said that South Carolina will not be allowed to host sports championship events until the flag is removed.

In Mississsippi, the state flag has included the Southern Cross since 1894. Activists have been trying to eliminate this element from the flag for many years. In 1983, African-American students at the University of Mississippi had asked school officials to stop using the Southern Cross as the school's official symbol. University officials soon lowered the rebel flags that flew over the campus. After that, black leaders in Mississippi called for removal of the flag atop the Capitol as well.

In January 2001 then-

> ## Make Connections
>
> In many communities in the South, March 4 is celebrated as "Confederate Flag Day." The battle flag is also flown in many southern cities on January 19— Robert E. Lee's birthday.

Governor Ronnie Musgrove signed a bill authorizing a *referendum* on the state flag. Voters would have an opportunity to decide whether they wanted to keep state's 1894 flag, or select a new design that substituted a blue field of stars for the Southern Cross.

For the next four months, the issue divided the citizens of Mississippi. One person who spoke on the issue was former Mississippi governor William Winter, whose grandfather had served in the Confederate Army. Winter said, "I share that deep sense of history; I understand how many feel. But I also feel a flag—a flag that represents a people, a whole state, ought to be a symbol of unity, not division."

The Confederate flag is often flown proudly by hate groups such as the Ku Klux Klan. These groups use the flag to intimidate African Americans and other minorities.

Mississippi flag, which still includes the Southern Cross, flies over the state Capitol in Jackson.

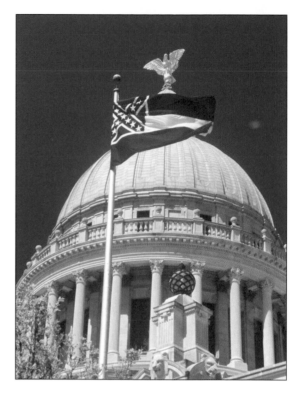

However, when citizens of Mississippi went to the polls, two-thirds voted to keep the 1894 flag. Their attitude, perhaps, can be summed up in the words of respected Civil War historian Shelby Foote, an author from Mississippi. "I'm for the Confederate flag now and forever," Foote said. "Many among the finest people this country has ever produced died in that war."

Text-Dependent Question
Which U.S. state removed the Confederate battle flag from its state flag in 2003?

Research Project
Georgia adopted a flag that included the Southern Cross in 1956, and South Carolina began flying the Confederate battle flag over the state capitol in 1962. What events that occurred in American society during the 1950s and 1960s probably inspired these changes? What did the state governments hope to accomplish by display Confederate symbols?

Chronology

1860 Abraham Lincoln elected president in November; in December Southern states begin declaring their intent to secede and form the Confederate States of America.

1861 Stars and Bars flag is raised above the state capitol in Montgomery, Alabama, on March 4; Civil War begins on April 12.

1863 Confederate Congress replaces the Stars and Bars with the Stainless Banner as the official flag of the Confederacy on May 1.

1865 A red bar is added to the Stainless Banner on March 8; on April 9, General Robert E. Lee surrenders to General Ulysses S. Grant at Appomattox, Virginia; the Confederate raider *Shenandoah* lowers the battle flag on November 6.

1894 Legislators in Mississippi adopt a state flag featuring the Southern Cross in the upper left corner on February 7.

1956 Georgia adopts a state flag that includes the Southern Cross on July 1.

1962 The South Carolina Legislature orders the Southern Cross flown atop the Capitol next to the state flag.

1983 Black students at the University of Mississippi convince school officials to drop the Southern Cross as the symbol of the university.

2000 The Southern Cross is removed from the South Carolina Capitol dome on July 1; it is displayed instead at a cemetery for Confederate soldiers on the Capitol grounds.

2001 Georgia adopts a new state flag featuring a small and less prominent Southern Cross on January 31.

2003 Georgia flag redesigned again to eliminate Southern Cross.

2008 A marker declaring Fairfax, Virginia, the birthplace of the Confederate battle flag is dedicated on April 12.

Series Glossary

capstone—a stone used at the top of a wall or other structure.

cornerstone—the first stone placed at a spot where two walls meet, usually considered the starting point of construction.

dome—an element of architecture that resembles the hollow upper half of a sphere.

edifice—a large building with an imposing appearance.

facade—the decorative front of a building.

foundation—the stone and mortar base built below ground that supports a building, bridge, monument, or other structure.

hallowed—holy, consecrated, sacred, or revered.

keystone—the architectural piece at the crown of a vault or arch which marks its apex, locking the other pieces into position.

memorial—something designed to help people remember a person or event in history.

obelisk—a shaft of stone that tapers at the peak.

pantheon—a public building containing monuments to a nation's heroes.

pedestal—the base or support on which a statue, obelisk, or column is mounted.

portico—a roof supported by columns, usually extending out from a building.

rotunda—a large and high circular hall or room in a building, usually surmounted by a dome.

standard—a flag or banner that is adopted as an emblem or symbol by a nation.

symbol—an item that represents or stands for something else.

Further Reading

Baldwin, John, and Ron Powers. *Last Flag Down: The Epic Journey of the Last Confederate Warship*. New York: Random House, 2007.

Brown, Kent Masterson. *The Southern Cross: The Story of the Confederacy's First Battle Flag*. Gretna, La.: Pelican Publishing., 2014.

Coski, John M. *The Confederate Battle Flag: America's Most Embattled Emblem*. Cambridge, Mass.: Harvard University Press, 2006.

Cannon, Devereaux D. Jr. *The Flags of the Confederacy: An Illustrated History*. Gretna, La.: Pelican Publishing, 1997.

Davis, William C. *A Government of Our Own: The Making of the Confederacy*. New York: The Free Press, 1994.

Fleche, Andre M. *The Revolution of 1861: The American Civil War in the Age of Nationalist Conflict*. Chapel Hill: University of North Carolina Press, 2012.

Garrison, Webb. *Civil War Curiosities*. Nashville: Rutledge Hill, 1994.

Guelzo, Allen C. *Fateful Lightning: A New History of the Civil War and Reconstruction*. NEw York: Oxford University Press, 2012.

Levine, Bruce. *The Fall of the House of Dixie: The Civil War and the Social Revolution that Transformed the South*. New York: Random House, 2013.

O'Brien, Cormac. *Secret Lives of the Civil War: What Your Teachers Never Told You about the War Between the States*. Illus. by Monika Suteski. Philadelphia: Quirk Books, 2007.

Owen, Richard, and James Owen. *Generals at Rest*. Shippensburg, Pa.: White Mane Publishing Company, 1997.

Internet Resources

http://www.nava.org

Website of the North American Vexillogical Association, a
non-profit, scholarly organization dedicated to the study of
flags and their cultural, historical, political, and social signifi-
cance.

http://www.usflag.org/confederate.stars.and.bars.html

This site shows the changes in the Confederate flags between
1861 and 1865, and provides some history on the
Confederate States of America.

http://www.civilwar.org/

Find out about the battlefields of the Civil War, take quizzes,
and learn how you can help preserve the historic sites where
Civil War battles occurred.

http://www.pbs.org/civilwar/

This companion website to the influential documentary by
Ken Burns includes images of original Civil War photographs,
historical documents, maps of key battles, research information, and more.

http://memory.loc.gov/ammem/cwphtml/cwphome.html

View images of more than 1,000 photographs of Civil War
military personnel, preparations for battle, after-effects of battles, and portraits of Confederate and Union officers.

Publisher's Note: The websites listed on this page were active at the time of
publication. The publisher is not responsible for websites that have changed
their address or discontinued operation since the date of publication. The
publisher reviews and updates the websites each time the book is reprinted.

Index

Index

Picture Credits

page
1: used under license from Shutterstock, Inc.
3: used under license from Shutterstock, Inc.
8: Hulton/Archive
12: Library of Congress
16: Hulton/Archive
18: Library of Congress
20: Library of Congress
22: Library of Congress
24: © Pidcock Press
26: © Pidcock Press
28: used under license from Shutterstock, Inc.
31: Hulton/Archive
32: Library of Congress
33: © Pidcock Press
34: Hulton/Archive
37: used under license from Shutterstock, Inc.
38: Hulton/Archive
40: Hulton/Archive
41: used under license from Shutterstock, Inc.

Contributors

BARRY MORENO has been librarian and historian at the Ellis Island Immigration Museum and the Statue of Liberty National Monument since 1988. *The Statue of Liberty Encyclopedia* (2000), *The Encyclopedia of Ellis Island* (2004), *Ellis Island's Famous Immigrants* (2008), and *The Ellis Island Quiz Book* (2011). He also co-edited a scholarly study on world migration called *Leaving Home: Migration Yesterday and Today* (2011). His biography has been included in *Who's Who Among Hispanic Americans*, *The Directory of National Park Service Historians*, *Who's Who in America*, and *The Directory of American Scholars*. Mr. Moreno lives in New York City.

HAL MARCOVITZ has written more than 100 books for young readers. He lives in Chalfont, Pennsylvania, with his wife, Gail. They have two grown daughters, Ashley and Michelle.

Harris County Public Library
Houston, Texas